caring
for us

I am a
Dentist

Deborah Chancellor

W

FRANKLIN WATTS
LONDON • SYDNEY

First published in 2010
by Franklin Watts

Copyright © Franklin Watts 2010

Franklin Watts
338 Euston Road
London NW1 3BH

Franklin Watts Australia
Level 17/207 Kent Street
Sydney, NSW 2000

Series editor: Jeremy Smith
Art director: Jonathan Hair
Design: Elaine Wilkinson
Photography: Chris Fairclough

Every attempt has been made to clear copyright. Should there be any inadvertent omission please
apply to the publisher for rectification.

Thanks to Chris, Donna, Katharine, Angela, Lily, Archie, Tracy, Connor, Scarlett, Louis and
all the staff at Broxbourne Dental Care.

Dewey number: 617.6

ISBN: 978 0 7496 9514 9

Printed in China

Franklin Watts is a division of Hachette Children's Books,
an Hachette UK company.
www.hachette.co.uk

Contents

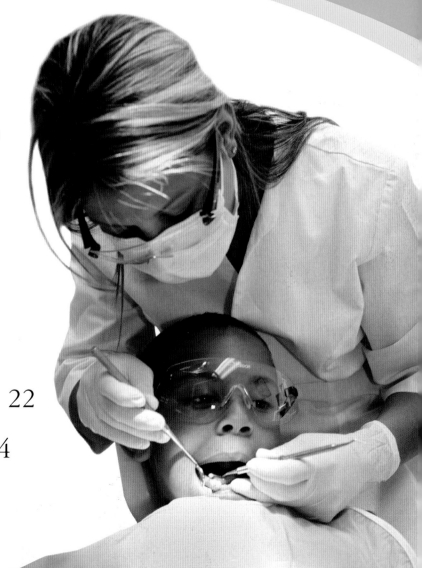

Words in **bold** are in the glossary on page 24.

My job

I am a dentist.
I check people's
teeth, to see if
they are strong
and healthy.

What do you think?

Why do
people go to
the dentist?

4

I work at a **dental surgery** in a town called Broxbourne.

At reception

People who want to see me have to phone the receptionist at the surgery to make an appointment.

The receptionist gives me a list
of my patients for the day.

In my surgery

I have lots of special equipment in my room at the dental surgery.

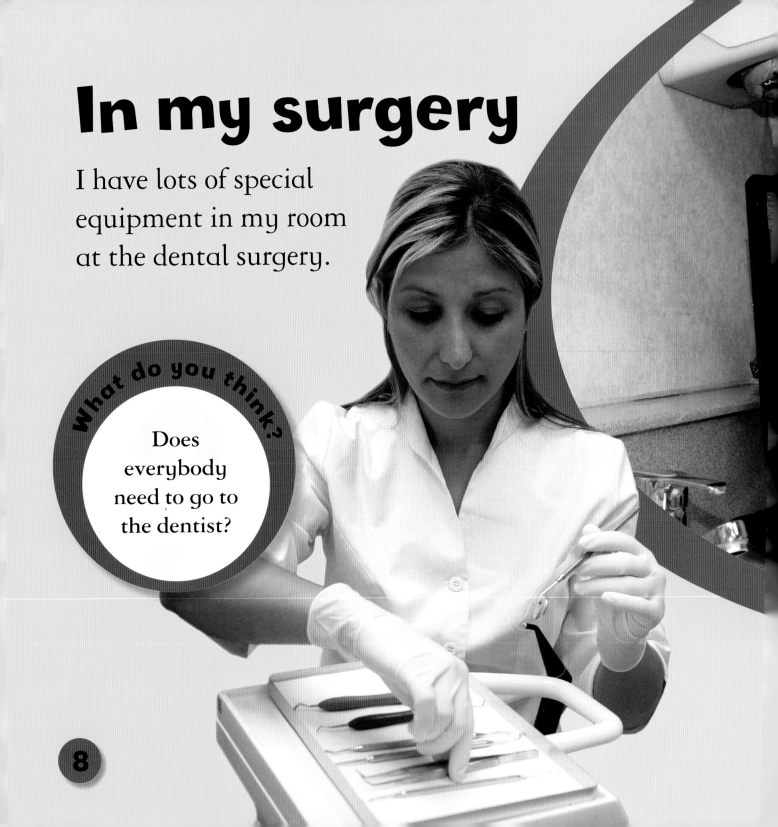

What do you think?

Does everybody need to go to the dentist?

All my patients' dental **records**
are on the computer.

The waiting room

Patients wait in the waiting room.
There are books for children to read.

My **dental nurse** fetches the patients when it is their turn to see me.

What do you think?

Do you like going to the dentist? Why?

11

My dental nurse

My dental nurse asks the patient to sit in a special chair. It moves up, down, forwards and backwards!

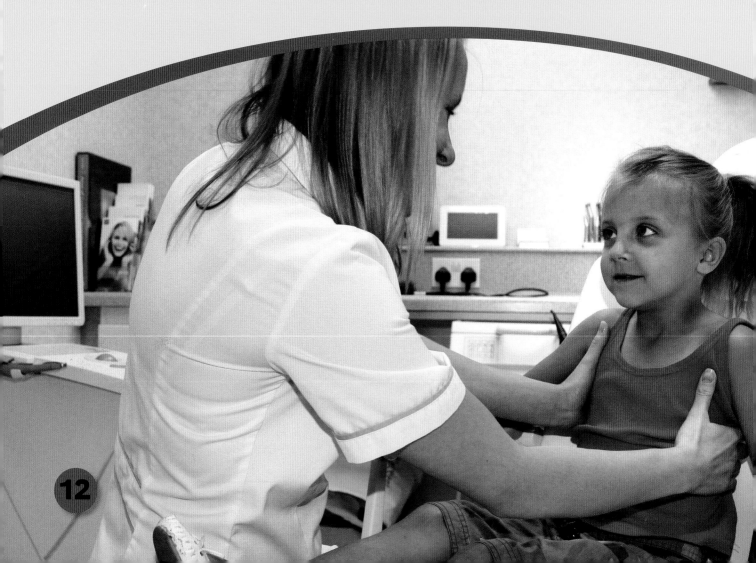

12

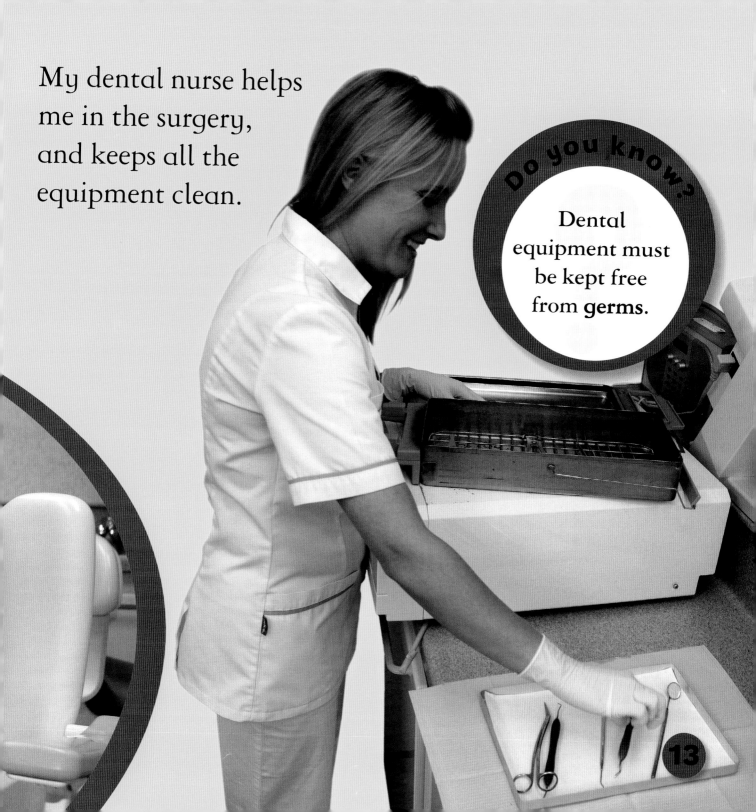

My dental nurse helps me in the surgery, and keeps all the equipment clean.

Do you know?

Dental equipment must be kept free from **germs**.

13

Check-up

I put a tiny camera in my patient's mouth, so I can see if their teeth and **gums** are healthy.

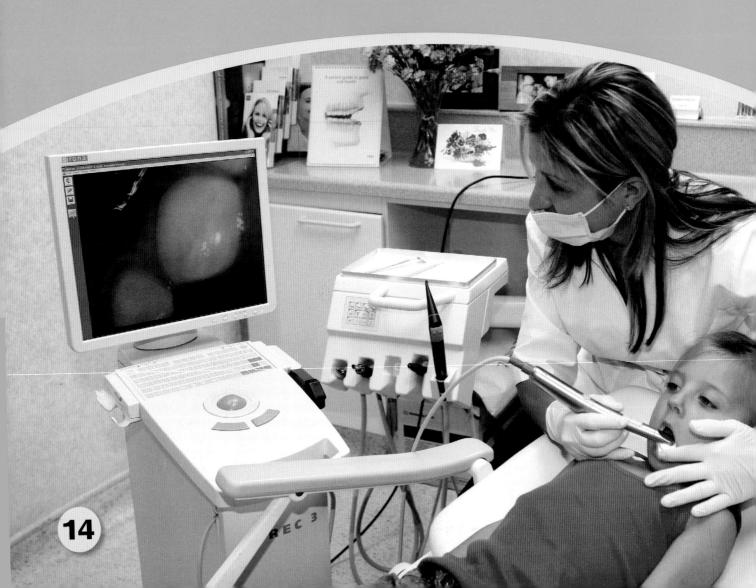

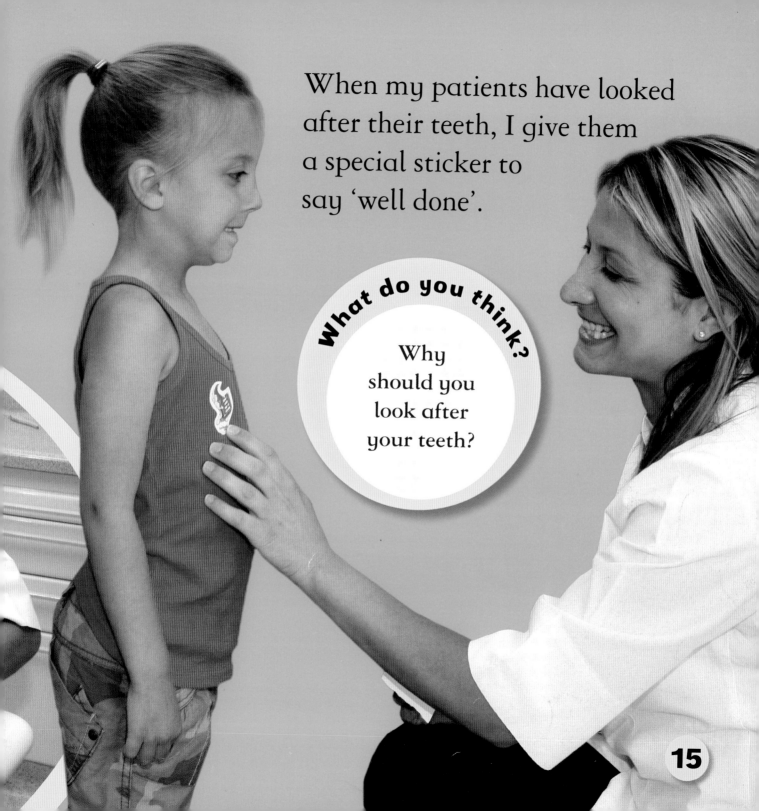

When my patients have looked after their teeth, I give them a special sticker to say 'well done'.

What do you think?

Why should you look after your teeth?

15

X-ray

I give some patients an **x-ray**, so I can see what **treatment** they need.

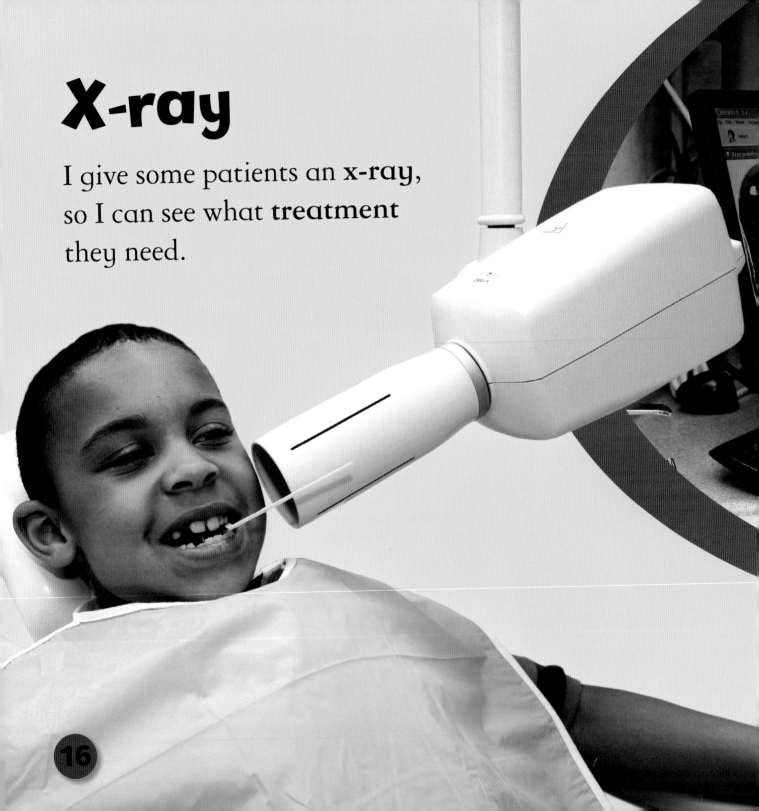

What do you think?

Would you like to work at a dental surgery one day? Why?

We look at the x-ray on the computer, and talk about it together.

Fillings

If a patient has **tooth decay**, I give them a filling. First, I prepare the mixture for the filling.

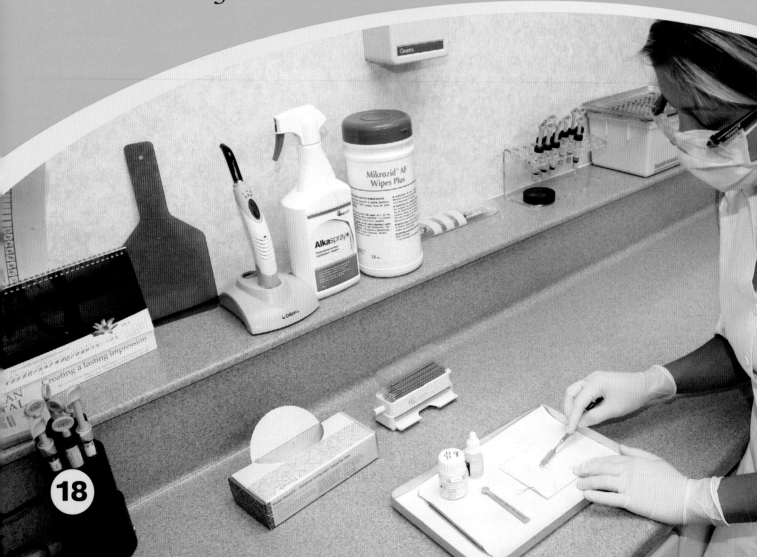

Then, I fill the hole in their tooth with the mixture. This stops the tooth from hurting.

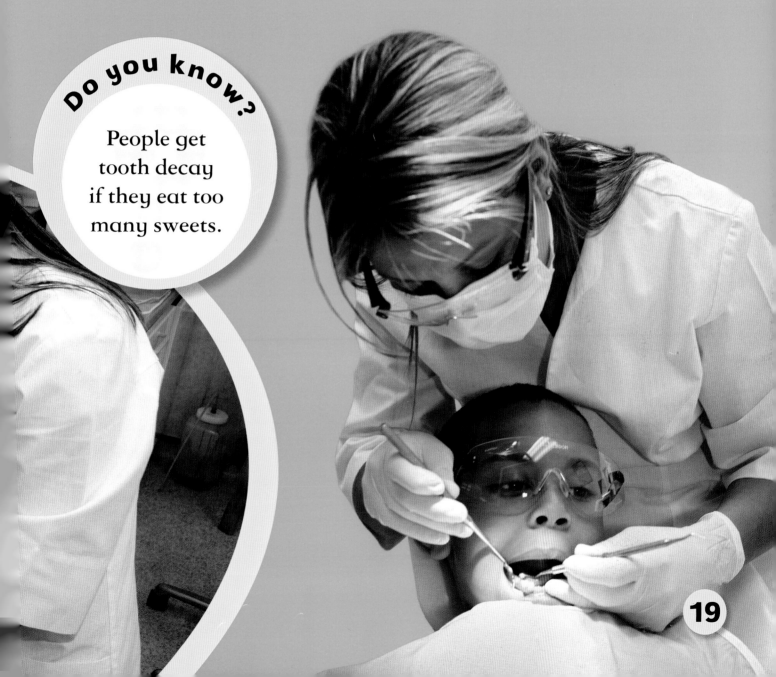

Do you know?

People get tooth decay if they eat too many sweets.

19

Accident!

Sometimes, people come to the surgery after an accident. They may have lost a tooth.

I see them straight away and give them **emergency** treatment.

What do you think?

What should you do if you break a tooth?

21

Look after your teeth

Learn how to clean your teeth properly. Brush your teeth every morning and evening.

What do you think?

Why are fizzy drinks bad for your teeth?

22

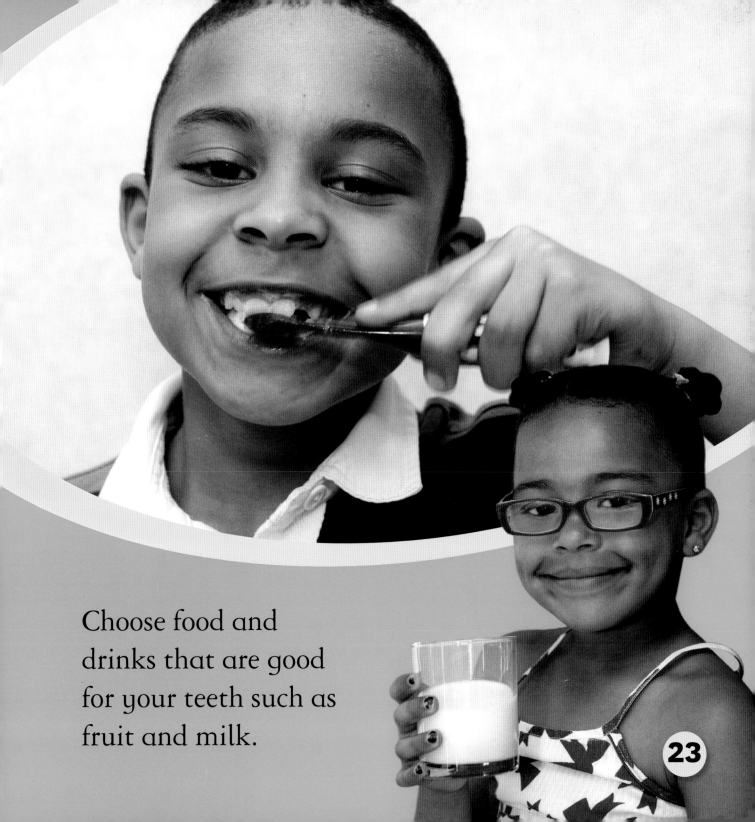

Choose food and drinks that are good for your teeth such as fruit and milk.

23

Glossary

dental nurse someone who helps dentists in a surgery

dental records information about your teeth and gums

dental surgery a place where dentists work

emergency a sudden, dangerous situation

germs things that cause disease

gums the part of your mouth that holds your teeth

tooth decay part of a tooth that is rotting away

treatment the care you are given to make you better

x-ray a photo that shows your bones and teeth

Index

START-UP
ART AND DESIGN

WHAT IS SCULPTURE?

Louise and Richard Spilsbury

Evans

Published by Evans Brothers Limited
2A Portman Mansions
Chiltern Street
London W1U 6NR

© Evans Brothers Limited 2007

Produced for Evans Brothers Limited by
White-Thomson Publishing Ltd.
Bridgewater Business Centre, 210 High Street,
Lewes, East Sussex BN7 2NH

Printed in China by WKT Co. Ltd.

Editor: Rachel Minay
Consultant: Susan Ogier Horwood, Art Education
Consultant specialising in Early Years and
Primary age range
Designer: Leishman Design

The rights of Louise and Richard Spilsbury to be
identified as the authors of this work have been asserted
by them in accordance with the Copyright, Designs and
Patents Act 1988.

British Library Cataloguing in Publication Data
Spilsbury, Louise and Richard
    What is sculpture? - (Start up art and design)
    1. Sculpture - Juvenile literature
    I. Title II. Spilsbury, Richard, 1963-
    730

    ISBN-13: 9780237533977

Acknowledgements:
Special thanks to Ms J. Arundell and pupils at Mayfield
Primary School, Hanwell, West London, for their help
and involvement in the preparation of this book.

Picture Acknowledgements:
Alamy pp. 5l (The Photolibrary Wales), 14 (Mike
Kipling Photography), 20 (Jenny Matthews); Bridgeman
Art Library pp. 8t, 16; Corbis pp. 5r (Richard T.
Nowitz), 6 (Bruce Burkhardt); Chris Fairclough pp.
cover (all), title page, 7l&r, 9l&r, 11, 13t, 15, 17 (all),
18l&r, 19, 21; iStockphoto.com p. 12 (all);
Shutterstock.com p. 4.

Artwork:
Amy Sparks p. 13b; Tech-Set Ltd p.10.

Contents

What is sculpture?

A sculpture is a work of art.
It is often a solid shape,
not flat like a painting.
Some are huge,
others are tiny.

◀ This sculpture is
called The Angel of
the North. It is 20
metres high – that's
taller than four
double-decker buses!

sculpture solid

Sculptures are often made of strong materials, such as metal, stone or wood. But they can be made from all kinds of materials.

▲ How long do you think this ice sculpture might last?

◄ We can see sculptures in galleries, town squares, parks and even our homes.

materials   galleries

Sculpting people

Sculptures of people take many different forms. French sculptor Auguste Rodin made structures that are solid and life-size or larger.

◀ What emotion does this figure's pose suggest? If he could talk, what do you think he would say to you?

sculptor   life-size   emotion

▲ Joe's class is going to make wire sculptures of people in different poses. The children take photos of each other. How will this help them?

▶ The children twist and bend wire into people shapes.

"I pressed the feet into clay to make my figure stand up."

pose   twist   bend   clay   7

Animal sculptures

▶ This is a sculpture of a stalking wolf. How does the sculptor make the wolf look as if it is moving?

How would you describe this sculpture in a letter to a friend to help them imagine it clearly?

▶ Zoe's class makes a spider diagram about the sculpture. What would you add to it?

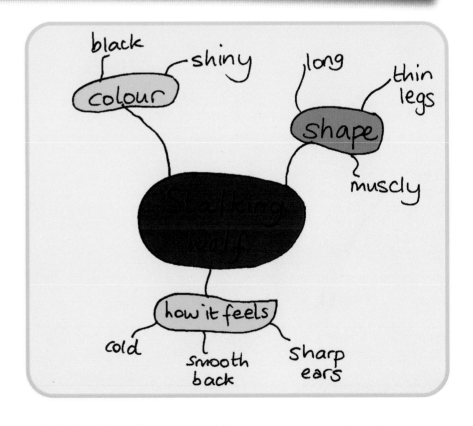

black — shiny

colour

long — thin legs

shape

muscly

Stalking wolf

how it feels

cold

smooth back

sharp ears

8   spider diagram   models   sketches

The children make clay animals. They look at models and draw sketches to help them make their sculptures more realistic.

▲ They make a clay body and then add the head and legs. James is rolling out a tail for his tiger.

▲ Zoe presses tools into the surface of the clay to make a pattern for her cheetah's back.

realistic   tools   surface

Card construction

Sculptures are formed by putting different shapes and spaces together in particular ways. Ben and his class construct a sculpture from different pieces.

Cylinder Cuboid Circle

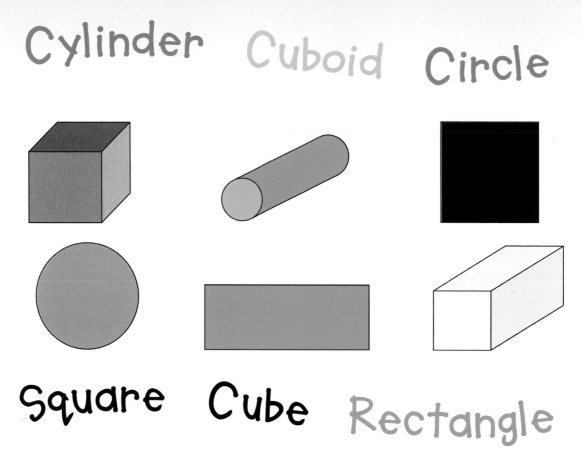

Square Cube Rectangle

First they make geometric card shapes. Can you match the words to the shapes?

construct geometric

The children think carefully about where to put the pieces. They try the shapes in different positions to create an interesting and balanced sculpture.

▲ The pieces in this sculpture are joined together with glue. What other methods of joining can you use?

positions   balanced   joined

Art from nature

Nature makes sculptures, too! The sea carves sand, wood and shells into interesting forms.

sand and seaweed

driftwood

shells

▲ How would these natural sculptures feel to touch?

Tip: When you are out, collect some natural objects for a sculpture, but only take fallen or dead materials.

carves   forms   research

► **Max and Neela research the artist Andy Goldsworthy. He often uses natural materials such as leaves and petals. Why does he take photos of these temporary sculptures?**

◄**Neela made her own temporary work of art. She made a relief collage by arranging natural objects on card.**

temporary   relief collage

Junk art

▶ This sculpture is made from reclaimed parts of electronic equipment. It represents the electronic waste one person makes in a lifetime.

How much waste does your family throw away each week? How much do you reuse or recycle?

reclaimed   represents   waste

▼ Dominic's class collects used materials for a sculpture. They make a junk art dragon.

wire and old fabric

old CDs

cereal boxes

egg box

What other reclaimed items did they use? What kind of junk sculpture will you make?

reuse   recycle

Casting sculptures

Every culture makes sculptures of some kind. This bronze head was made in Africa around 500 years ago.

► Big bead necklaces were only worn by royalty. The head is wearing a crown. The crown has strings of valuable beads too.

Sculptures like this are made by casting. Casting means making something in a mould.

culture   bronze   casting

Katy is making a cast sculpture. First she presses shapes into clay with tools and objects like shells. These are her moulds. Next she will pour plaster into the moulds.

► When the plaster sets hard, the sculpture is taken out of the plastic tray. Katy paints the sculpture to look like bronze.

mould   plaster   sets

Sculpture school

Sculptures can brighten up surroundings. An artist helped this school make a sculpture trail in the grounds.

◀ One class used the theme 'Africa'. Individual pieces were painted and joined together to make totem poles.

▶ This lion was made from clay. The features were carved while the clay was wet.

theme   totem poles   features

▼ The school also made a willow installation. Willow canes were planted in the ground and then bent and woven together to make an igloo and tunnel.

How do you think the sculptures improved the school environment?

installation   environment

Sculpture settings

Many sculptures are **displayed** in galleries. In a gallery, you can look at a sculpture from different **angles**.

▶ How do you think it feels to stand beneath this sculpture?

displayed   angles

It is useful to talk about how you feel about your own and other people's work. One sculpture can **communicate** different **ideas** to different people.

communicate ideas

Further information for

New words listed in the text:

angles	construct	geometric	plaster	research	surface
balanced	culture	ideas	pose	reuse	temporary
bend	displayed	installation	positions	sculptor	theme
bronze	emotion	joined	realistic	sculpture	tools
carves	environment	life-size	reclaimed	sets	totem poles
casting	features	materials	recycle	sketches	twist
clay	forms	models	relief collage	solid	waste
communicate	galleries	mould	represents	spider diagram	

Possible Activities

PAGES 4-5

The children could sort 2D and 3D objects to help them think about the differences.

Think about why different materials are used. When visiting outdoor sculptures, children should think about why metals such as bronze are used (long-lasting). What might weather do to outdoor sculptures?

PAGES 6-7

To help them with their wire sculptures, children could look at the wire figures of Alberto Giacometti. How do the sculptures make them feel? What are the figures doing? How does the fact they are modelled in wire give them a very different feeling to Rodin's solid sculptures?

PAGES 8-9

The children could think about why artists choose particular materials to work with. They might choose wood, so they can make certain marks in it or cut it in a certain way. Children could also discuss ways of getting inspiration and background material from which to work. They could visit a zoo, take photos or make sketches of animals, or study other animal sculptures for ideas. Many sculptures are carved, not modelled. At http://www.tate.org.uk/learning/kids/zoomroom/soapcarving/ there are ideas for making a soap sculpture based on Barbara Hepworth's sculptures.

PAGES 10-11

Children could first work in pairs to make sculptures out of plastic linking shapes. When making an abstract sculpture, be clear that when an artist creates an apparently random form they actually make many careful decisions about the end result and experiment before welding or joining the pieces together. You could look at the work of British sculptor Anthony Caro who used shapes and colours to make interesting abstract sculptures. Children could work individually on a sculpture like this, using materials such as lollipop sticks, pipe cleaners and straws.

Parents and Teachers

PAGES 12-13
When on a nature walk, the children can think about what they can smell and see, and the textures they can feel.
At the beach or wood, get the children to make ephemeral pieces of art themselves, such as sculptures made of sand or piled leaves. This could lead to discussions about the beauty of our fragile world, and how nature is constantly shifting and changing. Children could also make a nature mobile from found items such as driftwood, twigs, shells and cones. They will need to think about balance and symmetry to make the mobile work.

PAGES 14-15
Under supervision, children could take apart or use dismantled washing machines and other electronic equipment to make their own version of the WEEE sculpture.
Children could make a sculpture from reclaimed materials to stand near a recycling station to encourage people to think about recycling and to cover up unsightly bins.
Children could explore some of the sculptures Picasso made using junk items, such as a monkey with a toy car for a face.

PAGES 16-17
Viewing sculpture in relief on buildings could help with the cast model work. This could also link with a science project, such as one on skeletons, as children could use (clean) animal bones to create moulds too.

PAGES 18-19
For an interesting fact sheet about willow sculpture and how to do it, see: www.schoolsgarden.org.uk/resources/20willow.pdf

PAGES 20-21
If possible, arrange a visit to a gallery, ideally with the help of a gallery guide who can offer the children some insight into the

Further Information
BOOKS FOR CHILDREN
Sculpting (Action Art) by Isabelle Thomas (Raintree, 2005)

What Is a Sculpture? (Art's Alive) by Ruth Thomson (Franklin Watts, 2005)

Sculpture (First Discovery/Art) by Jean-Philippe Chabot (Moonlight Publishing Ltd, 2005)

Sculpture (Let's Start Art!) by Sue Nicholson (QED Publishing, 2005)

The Life & Work of Auguste Rodin by Jayne Woodhouse (Heinemann, 2001)

The Life & Work of Henry Moore by Sean Connolly and Jayne Woodhouse (Heinemann, 2001)

WEBSITES
http://www.sculpture.org.uk/homepage/
http://www.tate.org.uk
http://schools.becta.org.uk/
http://www.nga.gov/kids/kids.htm

sculptures and suggest new ways of seeing the art on display. This will also help the children think about the way they display their own sculptures and the significance of naming the sculptures. At the gallery, they could think about what questions they want to ask about a piece, such as why an artist chose a particular medium, and think about giving visitors to their own gallery this kind of information. The children could take photos of their sculpture work and load them onto the school website themselves, with descriptions of the processes involved and their feelings about the projects.

Index